PHILOSOPHY OF GOD,
AND THEOLOGY

BERNARD J. F. LONERGAN, S. J.

PHILOSOPHY OF GOD, AND THEOLOGY

The Relationship between Philosophy of God and the functional Specialty, Systematics

St. Michael's Lectures
Gonzaga University, Spokane

The inaugural lectures, 1972
with a foreword by Patrick B. O'Leary, S. J.

Darton, Longman & Todd
London

First published in Great Britain in 1973 by
Darton, Longman & Todd, Ltd
85 Gloucester Road, London SW7 4SU

© 1973 Bernard J. F. Longman, S.J.

ISBN 0 232 51234 5

Text set in 12/14 pt. Monotype Bembo, printed by letterpress,
and bound in Great Britain at The Pitman Press, Bath

CONTENTS

FOREWORD

In the fall of 1972, St. Michael's Jesuit School of Philosophy and Letters at Gonzaga University inaugurated the St. Michael's Lectures as a forum for outstanding international scholars to examine the question of God in modern thought. The theme for the lecture series is much the same as that of the famous Gifford Lectures, but the approach is not only philosophical but also theological.

The uniqueness lies primarily in the dynamic inherent in the structure of the series. A lecture in a tripartite form (over a three day period) is given each fall. As the series unfolds, each lecturer is to enter into dialogue with the immediately preceding lecturer and, to the extent that he wishes, he may respond to other former lecturers in the series. At the same time, each expands the discussion by his or her own creative contribution. As a result there will develop an ongoing exchange among thinkers of international reputation.

It is especially fortunate for the series that we could begin with a theologian who is recognized universally as one of the greatest thinkers of our times. In his inaugural Lecture, Fr. Bernard J. F. Lonergan, S.J., grapples with the problem of the relationship among religious experience, philosophy of God, and the area of systematic theology. In doing so he challenges the separation that has grown up between the philosophical and the theological approaches to the God problematic. The position that he espouses lays the foundation for what promises to be a very fruitful dialogue.

It is only fitting that recognition be given to those who have been so instrumental in bringing to reality what might have been so easily just another good idea: to Fr. Bernard J. Tyrrell, S.J., and Fr. William F. J. Ryan, S.J., for seeing the creative possibilities of an ongoing dialogue and for then helping to bring these possibilities to fruition, and to the Jesuits of St. Michael's for the innumerable ways that they have contributed their assistance.

We are happy to make available to a larger public than those who could attend the lectures this exciting beginning of an exchange among scholars of the highest quality on the question that touches us most profoundly, the question of God.

Patrick B. O'Leary, S.J.
Rector of St. Michael's Institute,
Gonzaga University.

INTRODUCTION

While the title of these three lectures is rather long, its terms are not perhaps self-explanatory. I shall begin by giving some indication of the meaning of the terms. I then shall outline the topics to be treated in the several lectures.

By "philosophy of God" is meant thought and affirmations or negations concerning God that are not logically derived from revealed religion. In this statement the operative word is "logically." For in my opinion the notion of a philosophy of God pertains to a context in which classicism and conceptualism are taken for granted as self-evident. By a classicist I mean a person for whom the rhetorician or orator of Isocrates or Cicero represents the fine flower of human culture. By a conceptualist I mean a person that is a keen logician, that is extremely precise in his use of terms, and that never imagined that the meaning of terms varied with the acts of understanding that they expressed.

By the functional specialty, "systematics," is meant the effort of human understanding to gain some insight into revealed truths. Systematics, then, differs radically from philosophy of God. It presupposes revealed truths. The two, then, are quite distinct. But there is a further difference. Philosophy of God aims at proving the existence of God and his several attributes. But the functional specialty, systematics, does not attempt to prove anything. That revealed truths are revealed and true, is established in other functional specialties. Systematics takes over the truths from the other specialties and its aim is, not to find further proofs, but to understand as best it can what has already been established to be so.

There remains a third term. Our principal topic is, not philosophy of God, not the functional specialty, systematics, but the relationship between the two. That relationship we shall contend is distinction but not separation. The two are quite distinct. In an age dominated by classicism and conceptualism, the two should be separated. But conditions that obtained in the past no longer prevail. Consequently, there no longer is any reason to separate the two, to have philosophy of God taught by philosophers in a department of philosophy while the functional specialty, systematics, is taught by theologians in a department of theology or of religious studies.

So much for the meaning of the title of these lectures. By philosophy of God is meant knowledge of God that is not logically derived from revealed religion. By the functional specialty, systematics, is meant a specialty that receives revealed truths from other specialties and seeks some imperfect understanding of them. Finally, the relationship between the two at all times is that they are quite distinct. Under the peculiar circumstances of recent centuries the relationship has been thought to be that the the two should be kept quite separate. At the present time it has been my contention in my recent book, *Method in Theology*,[1] that the two while distinct should not be separated. I may add that I believe Karl Rahner to be of the same opinion though not, of course, for the same reasons.

With the terms in the title explained, it is fairly obvious that the topic of the first of these three lectures should be the philosophy of God, that the topic of the second lecture should be the functional specialty, systematics, and that the topic of the third lecture should be the relationship between the two.

First of all, then, we are to attempt to grasp what is meant by philosophy of God. As might be expected, there are as many

[1] London: Darton, Longman and Todd, and New York: Herder and Herder, 1972.

meanings to the phrase as there are philosophic contexts in which
t is uttered. Our basic concern, accordingly, will be an attempt to
grasp certain fundamental contours relevant to an understanding
of variations in philosophic context.

PHILOSOPHY OF GOD

IN this title there are two words whose meaning is somewhat obscure. The first of these is "philosophy," and the second is "God."

The obscurity in question is not, of course, that people have no notion of what is meant by these terms. It is that people have different notions at different times and places. Here the underlying fact is what I have named differentiations of consciousness. The human mind is ever the same, but the techniques it employs develop over time.

A first differentiation of consciousness arises when the infant learns to speak. He or she had been living in a world of immediacy, a world that contained only what could be seen, heard, touched, tasted, smelt, felt. But learning to speak involves an enormous extension of the world of immediacy. It includes not only the present and factual but also the absent, the past, the future, the merely possible or ideal or normative or fantastic. In entering the world mediated by meaning one moves out of one's immediate surroundings towards a world revealed through the memories of other men, through the common sense of community, through the pages of literature, through the labors of scholars, through the investigations of scientists, through the experience of saints, through the meditations of philosophers and theologians.[2]

A second differentiation is observable in the transition from a primitive language to that of an ancient high civilization and,

[2] *Method in Theology*, p. 28.

again, from the language of practical achievement to the language that has developed a high literature.

A primitive language has little difficulty in expressing all that can be pointed out or directly perceived or directly represented. But the generic cannot be directly pointed out or perceived or represented. So in Homer there were words for such specific activities as glancing, peering, staring, but no generic word for seeing. Again, in various American languages of the aborigines one cannot simply say that the man is sick; one also has to retail whether he is near or far, whether he can or cannot be seen; and often the form of the sentence will also reveal his place, position, and posture. Again, the temporal cannot be pointed out or directly perceived or represented. Time involves a synthesis of all events in a single continuum of earlier and later. So an early language may have an abundance of tenses but they are found to mean, not a synthesis of temporal relationships, but different kinds of action. Thirdly, the subject and his inner experience lie not on the side of the perceived but on the side of the perceiving. One can point to the whole man or to some part of him, but one cannot point out the pointer. So possessive pronouns develop before personal pronouns, for what one possesses can be pointed out, but oneself as a subject is another story. Again, inner processes of thinking or deliberating are represented in Homer, not as inner processes, but as personalized interchanges. The Homeric heroes do not think or deliberate; they converse with a god or goddess, with their horse or with a river, with some part of themselves such as their heart or their temper. Finally, the divine is the objective of questioning our questioning. It cannot be perceived or imagined. But it can be associated with the object or event, the ritual or the recitation that occasion religious experience, and so there arise the hierophanies.[3]

Early language, then, is abundant on the spatial, the specific, the external, the human, but is weak on the temporal, the generic, the internal, and the divine. The long transition from primitive fruit-

[3] *Method in Theology*, pp. 87 f.

gatherers, hunters, and fishers to the large-scale agriculture of the temple states and later the ancient high civilizations brought with it a vast enrichment of language. For men do not do things without first talking about them and planning them, and so there had to be a linguistic development equal to the great works of irrigation, the vast structures of stone or brick, the armies and navies, the complicated processes of bookkeeping, and the beginnings of arithmetic, geometry, and astronomy. But the discovery and the objectification of the human spirit were achieved most notably by the Greeks. On a first level there was the literary revelation of man to himself. Homeric simile drew on the characteristics of inanimate nature and of plants and animals to illuminate and objectify and distinguish the varied springs of action in epic heroes. The lyric poets went on to an exploration of personal feelings. The dramatists exhibited human decisions, their conflicts and interplay, and their consequences. Within the literary tradition there occurred reflection on human knowledge. The epic writers explained their knowledge by referring to the muses. For Homer they see everything, and so the bard can describe the past as though he was an eye-witness. For Hesiod they do not inspire but teach, and they teach not only truth but also falsehood. As Hesiod proposed to tell the truth about the struggle in which man ekes out his livelihood, Xenophanes criticized anthropomorphic conceptions and representations of the gods, and Hecataeus maintained that the stories of the Greeks were many and foolish, that man's knowledge was not the gift of the gods, that stories of the past were to be judged by everyday experience, and that knowledge is acquired by planned and deliberate investigation. This empirical interest lived on in Herodotus, in the physicians, and in the physicists. But Heraclitus insisted that mere amassing of information did not make men grow in intelligence. There is an intelligence, a logos, that steers through all things. It is found in god and man and beast, the same in all, though in different degrees in each. To know it is wisdom.[4]

[4] *Method in Theology*, pp. 89 ff.

3

We have been distinguishing a first and a second differentiation of consciousness: the first occurs when one learns to talk; the second occurs when one learns a language rich and varied and supple enough to portray men in all their complexity. It is this second differentiation that leads to the third. Socrates made it his purpose to study, not the universe, but mankind. In Plato's early dialogues he is seeking universal definitions of temperance or courage or knowledge or justice. He explains over and over just what a universal definition is. He admits that he does not know the answers to his own questions. He can show just where any proposed definition fails. But not many decades later Aristotle in the *Nicomachean Ethics* was able to define all the virtues and to contrast with each, vices that sinned by excess and by defect. What, one may ask, enabled Aristotle to succeed where Socrates and his contemporaries had failed?

To this the answer is a third differentiation of consciousness. Aristotle was able to define because he moved beyond the ordinary language of common sense and the refinements brought to it by literary development into systematic thinking. He scrutinized words, listed their several meanings, selected the meanings that meshed together to constitute a basic perspective, and made this interlocking group of meanings the primitive terms and relations that provided the basis for derived definitions.

Let me illustrate this shift from ordinary and literary language from a more recent illustration. Sir Arthur Eddington spoke of his two tables. One was brown, rectangular, solid, heavy, plainly visible. The other was mostly empty space with only here and there some mysterious entity that at one moment had to be imagined as a wave and at another as a particle. In fact, of course, there were not two tables, but there were two quite distinct apprehensions of the same reality. The first of these apprehensions was the common-sense apprehension. The second was the systematic apprehension. On the basis of common-sense apprehension satisfactory universal definitions cannot be produced. This was

4

clear from the Socratic experiment, for every Athenian knew perfectly well the difference between temperance and gluttony, between courage and cowardice, between knowledge and ignorance, between justice and injustice. But it is one thing to know the meaning of words. It is quite another to be able to define that meaning. As our contemporary analysts keep repeating, one knows the meaning of a word when one is able to use it appropriately. But any word can be used appropriately in a variety of manners, and definition becomes possible only when a precise set of univocal and interlocking meanings has been selected, clarified, determined.

A further point must be made. While one may make one's entry into the world of systematic meaning by using the already familiar common-sense meanings of words, nonetheless one thereby is entering into a completely new world. We all have had experience of weight and momentum, but neither of these experiences, nor any other, is precisely what is meant by mass: weight is mg, momentum is mv, but mass is just the m. We all have had experience of heat and cold, but that experience does not coincide with what is meant by temperature. A wooden and a metal object in the same room will be of the same temperature, but one will feel warmer than the other. We all have experience of the endless conveniences provided by electricity, but that experience fails to yield a clue to Maxwell's equations for the electromagnetic field. To move into the systematic differentiation of consciousness does not merely involve the employment of a new set of technical meanings. It involves a new method of inquiry, a new style of understanding, a different mode of conception, a more rigorous manner of verification, and an unprecedented type of social group that can speak to one another in the new way.

In general, a logical system has three characteristics. Its root is a set of basic terms and basic relations, where the relations fix the terms, and the terms fix the relations. By means of the basic terms and basic relations other derived terms and derived relations may be defined. Through the derived terms and relations the whole system may be related to the data of experience.

Such general characteristics, however, may be found in quite different contexts. Three such contexts merit our attention: there is the Aristotelian type based on a metaphysics; there is the modern type based on empirical science; there is the transcendental type based on intentionality analysis.

Aristotle conceived system as a permanent achievement. It was to be an expression of truth and, what once is true, always is true. Further, he conceived that basic terms and basic relations were metaphysical, and accordingly that the terms proper to physics, psychology, and similar sciences were to be simply further determinations of the basic terms and basic relations set forth in metaphysics. Finally, in his *Posterior Analytics* he conceived science as a deduction from first principles that expressed objective necessity. It is to be noted, however, that neither Aristotle himself nor his disciple, Thomas Aquinas, went out of their way to provide their work with necessary first principles; they were content to do what they could. In contrast, fourteenth-century theologians paid enormous attention to necessary truth. They were forever distinguishing between what God could do absolutely and what he may be expected to do in this ordered universe. Finally, since God absolutely could do anything that did not involve a strict contradiction, there rapidly followed first scepticism and then decadence.

A second type of system is found in modern science. Up to the present century it felt itself in possession of necessary truth: not only were there the necessary laws of physics but also the iron laws of economics. A first breach in this wall was effected by the nineteenth-century discovery of non-Euclidean geometry. This was further enlarged by Gödel's theorem that a deductive system, if not trivial, will either be incoherent or incomplete: incoherent if the same proposition can be both proved and disproved; incomplete, if questions arise in the system but cannot be solved within it. The modesty engendered in mathematicians was extended to physics by the introduction and acceptance of quantum theory. Laplace's determinist world, in which in theory any world situation could be deduced from any other, was replaced by a fundamental indeterminism covered over by statistical regularities.

The systems, then, of modern science differ from the Aristotelian type in three manners. First of all, they fought to liberate science from domination by metaphysics. Instead of borrowing their basic terms and relations from metaphysics, they worked out their own basic terms and relations, such as mass, temperature, the electromagnetic field, the equations of quantum theory, the periodic table, the evoluntionary tree. Secondly, they discovered that the intelligibility they attained was the intelligibility, not of what must be so, but of what can be so and happens in fact to be verified. A science, in which discoveries have to be verified, is a science that discovers not necessities but possibilities. Where Aristotelian system aims to present truth, modern empirical systems aim at an ever fuller understanding and so at an asymptotic approach towards truth. Finally, modern science is more fully aware of the exigences of system. It does not believe that to reach systematic thinking it is enough to add to a word in ordinary language the appendage, "as such," *qua tale, kath' hauto;* Aristotle was not sufficiently aware of this pitfall, and much less were his fourteenth-century followers.

We have been contrasting two manners in which systematic thinking has been carried out, and we have now to advert to a third. Its basic terms denote the conscious and intentional operations that occur in human knowing. Its basic relations denote the conscious dynamism that leads from some operations to others. Its derived terms and relations are the procedures of common sense, of mathematicians, of empirical scientists, of interpreters and historians, of philosophers and theologians. It begins from cognitional theory: What are you doing when you are knowing? It moves on to epistemology: Why is doing that knowing? It concludes with a metaphysics: What do you know when you do it?

It differs from Aristotelian system inasmuch as its basic terms and relations are not metaphysical but cognitional. It resembles modern science inasmuch as its basic terms and relations are not given to sense, but differs from modern science inasmuch as its basic terms and relations are given to consciousness. Unlike Aristotle and like modern science, its basic truths are not necessities but verified possibilities. Like modern science, its positions can be revised in the sense that they can be refined and filled out indefinitely; but unlike modern science, its basic structures are not open to radical revision, for they contain the conditions of any possible revision and, unless those conditions are fulfilled, revision cannot occur.[5]

I have spent so much time on the various systematic differentiations of consciousness because they are highly relevant not only to the conception of the philosophy of God but also to the functional specialty entitled systematics. But to these points I shall return. I now have to note the existence of what I have called the post-systematic differentiation of consciousness. The development of philosophic and scientific systems profoundly affects a culture. But if it modifies the outlook of most of the members in the culture, still it does not do so by transforming them into systematic thinkers. Systematic thinkers are relatively rare. But their achievement is diffused by the commentators, the teachers, the popularizers that illuminate, complete, transpose, similify. Some of the fruits of systematic thinking are enjoyed, but no real transition is effected from the everyday world mediated by common-sense meaning to the heady atmosphere of the world mediated by systematic meaning.

While other differentiations of consciousness might be described, it will meet present needs if we say something about the religious differentiation of consciousness. I have placed this differentiation

[5] Further properties of this type of system are outlined in the first chapter of *Method in Theology*.

in God's gift of his grace. That gift St. Paul described when he wrote that "...God's love has flooded our inmost heart through the Holy Spirit he has given us" (Rom. 5, 5). The power of that gift he described when he wrote: "For I am convinced that there is nothing in death or life, in the realm of spirits or superhuman powers, in the world as it is or in the world as it shall be, in the forces of the universe, in heights or depths—nothing in all creation that can separate us from the love of God in Christ Jesus our Lord" (Rom. 8, 38 f.). To the exercise of that gift we are commanded in both the Old Testament and the New: "Hear, O Israel, the Lord your God is the only Lord; love the Lord your God with all your heart, with all your soul, with all your mind, and with all your strength" (Mark 12, 29 f.; Deut. 6, 4 f.).

The exercise of the gift consists in acts of love, but the gift itself is a dynamic state that fulfills the basic thrust of the human spirit to self-transcendence. That fulfillment brings a deep-set joy that can remain despite humiliation, failure, privation, pain, betrayal, desertion. It is a fulfillment that brings a radical peace that the world cannot give. That joy and peace radiate in a love of one's neighbor equal to one's love of oneself; it abounds in acts of kindness, goodness, fidelity, gentleness, and self-control (Gal. 5: 22).

In itself and in its fruits the gift of God's love is conscious. But when I say that it is conscious, I do not mean that it is known. Human knowing is a compound of many different operations. It begins from internal or external experience. It goes on to inquiring, understanding, formulating, then to reflecting, weighing and marshalling the evidence, and finally to affirming or denying. Our conscious acts and states are just the raw materials of human knowing, and to effect the transition from the mere raw materials to the finished product is a long and difficult process.

Not only is the dynamic state of being in love conscious but it also is consciously unrestricted. What scripture commands, God's grace achieves, namely, a love that is with all one's heart and all one's soul and all one's mind and all one's strength. More-over, in the unrestricted character of the loving we discover that it is love of God, for it would be idolatry to love a creature in that absolute fashion.

Note, too, that this being in love does not presuppose or depend on any apprehension of God. It is God's free gift. He gives it not because we have sought and found him but to lead us on to seeking and finding him. As Blaise Pascal put it: one would not be seeking God, unless one had already found him.

It may be objected that we cannot love what we do not know, and I should grant that that generally is the case. Activities on the fourth level of human consciousness presuppose activities on the previous three levels. But God's gift is not something that we produce; it is something that we receive; it is a completion and fulfillment of our being from on high. It is, to repeat what I have already quoted from St. Paul, God's love flooding our inmost heart through the Holy Spirit he has given us.

Further, according to the thirteenth chapter of the first epistle to the Corinthians, charity is necessary for salvation. Again, by common consent, charity is sufficient for salvation. But, as theologians argue from the first epistle to Timothy, chapter two, verse four, God wills all men to be saved. Accordingly, he wills to give them all the necessary and sufficient condition for salvation. It follows that he gives all men the gift of his love, and so it further follows that there can be an element in all the religions of mankind that is at once profound and holy.

If I have concluded that there is a common element to all the religions of mankind, I must now add that there is a specific element proper to Christianity. Christianity involves not only the inward gift of being in love with God but also the outward expression of God's love in Christ Jesus dying and rising again. In the paschal mystery the love that is given inwardly is focused and inflamed, and that focusing unites Christians not only with Christ but also with one another.

We have been preparing the ground by discussing differentiations of consciousness. We have noted the differentiations occasioned by the infant's learning to talk, by the technology of the ancient high civilizations, by the objectification of man in the unfolding of Greek literature, by the threefold introduction of system, first in its Aristotelian form, then in the form of empirical science, and thirdly on the basis of intentionality analysis and, finally, we have adverted to the religious differentiation of consciousness—the differentiation that is of basic importance to the present inquiry.

For if it should happen that anyone accepted my views on the religious differentiation of consciousness, he would be led to conclude that Pascal's distinction between the god of the philosophers and the God of Abraham, Isaac, and Jacob need not be taken too seriously. For if both the philosopher and the theologian had experienced the religious differentiation of consciousness, then both would be seeking to know the same God even though they employed means that were quite distinct. Further, since it is highly desirable that there be no ambiguity about the god or God that the philosophy of God sought to know, there exists a preliminary reason for transferring the philosophy of God from the philosophy and into the theology department. For in the theology department there may exist functional specialties named dialectic and foundations that are calculated to reveal whether or not the religious differentiation of consciousness has occurred in any given individual.

A further consideration seems relevant to me. In chapter nineteen of my book, *Insight*,[6] there is outlined a philosophy of God. Now in Easter week in 1970 at St. Leo's near Tampa, Florida, there was held a congress—I must add that one of its prime movers was Fr. Bernard Tyrrell of this university—and among the topics discussed was that very chapter nineteen. The discussion was unfavorable. It was felt, I think, that that chapter did not at all

[6] London: Longmans, Green and Co., and New York: Philosophical Library, 1957.

fit into the direction in which earlier parts of the work had been moving. It seemed to be a mere survival, if not a piece of wreckage, from an earlier age.

At the time my response was brief and noncommittal. I recalled that I had been studying methods generally as a preparation for work on the method of theology. I had been informed that I was to be shipped to Rome the following year to teach theology at the Gregorian. I foresaw that my ultimate project would have to be postponed. I decided to round off what I had done and publish the result under the title, *Insight*. Chapter nineteen in that work was part of the process of rounding things off.

Now of course I can see that the main incongruity was that, while my cognitional theory was based on a long and methodical appeal to experience, in contrast my account of God's existence and attributes made no appeal to religious experience.

Further, *Insight* insists a great deal on the authenticity of the subject, on his need to reverse his counter-positions and develop his positions, on the importance, in brief, of intellectual conversion. But if *Method in Theology* may be taken as the direction in which *Insight* was moving, then that direction implies not only intellectual but also moral and religious conversion. One might claim that *Insight* leaves room for moral and religious conversion, but one is less likely to assert that the room is very well furnished.

More specifically, proof in any serious meaning of the term presupposes the erection of a system, in which all terms and relations have an exact meaning, and all procedures from some propositions to others are rigorous. But the system itself, in turn, has its presuppositions. It presupposes a horizon, a world-view, a differentiation of consciousness that has unfolded under the conditions and circumstances of a particular culture and a particular historical development.

Now this presupposition of horizon is not a logical presupposition from which conclusions are drawn. On the contrary, it is part of the subject's equipment if he is to understand the meaning of the terms, to grasp the validity of the arguments, to value the goal of the investigation. In the past and particularly in the Catholic past the existence of subjective differences were well known but they were considered to be of only subjective significance. Moreover, this view was sustained in two ways. On the one hand, there was the Aristotelian belief that there existed first principles that were necessary truths. On the other hand, there was a normative notion of culture. There were not acknowledged as many different cultures as there were differing sets of meanings and values informing different ways of life. That meaning of the word "culture" had not yet gained currency. To be cultured was to meet certain standards. One met them in the measure one had the right sort of education and so could follow right reason and be a man of good will.

The trouble with chapter nineteen in *Insight* was that it did not depart from the traditional line. It treated God's existence and attributes in a purely objective fashion. It made no effort to deal with the subject's religious horizon. It failed to acknowledge that the traditional viewpoint made sense only if one accepted first principles on the ground that they were intrinsically necessary and if one added the assumption that there is one right culture so that differences in subjectivity are irrelevant.

There emerges from this outline the distinction between different and opposed meanings of the phrase, "philosophy of God." There is an older meaning that considers philosophy in general and philosophy of God in particular to be so objective that it is independent of the mind that thinks it. There is a newer meaning that conceives objectivity to be the fruit of authentic subjectivity. On the former view philosophy of God need not be concerned with the philosophic subject. On the latter view philosophy of God must not attempt to prescind from the subject. This means that intellectual, moral, and religious conversion have to be taken into account.

Now there is no difficulty about theologians in a theology

department reflecting on specifically Christian religious experience, but there would be some difficulty in asking philosophers in a philosophy department to reflect on specifically Christian religious experience. Again, there is no difficulty about theologians in a theology department reflecting on Christian religious conversion and employing those reflections to determine the horizon of their theologizing. Nor is there any difficulty about theologians explaining why the god of the philosophers need not be different from the God of Abraham, Isaac, and Jacob. So there is some reason for suggesting that it may be possible and even reasonable to transfer philosophy of God into the functional specialty, systematics.

QUESTIONS AND ANSWERS

Question 1:

"In a lecture of yours, 'Dimensions of Meaning,' you state: '. . . once philosophy becomes existential and historical, once it asks about man, not in the abstract, not as he would be in some state of nature, but as in fact he is here and now in all the concreteness of his living and dying, the very possibility of the distinction [I presume you mean separation, in the light of the present lecture] between philosophy and theology vanishes.'[1] In the light of this quotation and certain implications of the present lecture, would you not now also hold that the separation, not the distinction, between a natural ethics and a Christian ethics, and between a natural philsophy of man and a theological anthropology should be abolished?"

Lonergan: "Right. My concern is with a state of culture. A theology mediates between a religion and a culture. Its function is to express in terms of the culture the significance and value of the religion. And it does it differently when you have a different culture. Modern science, modern scholarship, and modern philosophy—all three are quite different from what they were in the Greek world or in the medieval world or in the Renaissance period.

I taught theology for twenty-five years under impossible conditions. It was that the whole setup of the school was predicated upon things that were fine in the sixteenth-century, but you could not use modern scholarship properly the way things are lined up. Now, the divisions introduced by Christian Wolff *are* not sacrosanct. What is wanted is not philosophy in general, but first of all transcendental method: what's common to all method, what's the gound of all method (that's chapter one of *Method in Theology*); and an apprehension of the human good (that's chapter

---

[1] In *Collection*, ed. F. E. Crowe, S. J., London: Darton, Longman and Todd, and New York: Herder and Herder, 1967, p. 266.

15

two) so that we are able to say why religion is good; and an account of meaning and all its varieties and differences as a basis for interpretation in history and communication (that's chapter three); and what is religion (chapter four), what is the question about God.

And the question about God is much more important than the proof of God, because at the present time people deny that the question exists. So, just as doctrines includes not only the dogmas in the traditional sense of the Greek councils, and so on, but also moral doctrines, so systematics will include both types of doctrines. An introduction to ethics is in chapter two, but any detailed account of ethics—both the natural ethics and the Christian ethics—will be in the chapter on systematics."

Question 1 (Continued): "If you grant that the separation but not the distinction between natural ethics and a Christian ethics should be abolished, then in what functional specialty should 'natural ethics' be taught?"

Answer: "It comes into systematics the way philosophy of God comes into systematics. It should be introduced not only on that level. You have to set up your methodical foundations first. You have to say something in general about the human good, not just that the good is 'what everything seeks,' and leave it at that."

Question 1 (Continued): "How should the philosophy of man, then, be transported into systematics?"

Lonergan: "I think questions of detail are going to be solved by committees dealing with concrete problems. When I say that the formal object is settled by the method, I mean that distinctions and/or separations are determined by comparing and contrasting, not subjects, but methods."

Question 1 (Continued): "You would say, in other words, that the old distinctions between natural morality and Christian morality, between philosophy of man and Christian anthropology are artificial and wrong, and there has to be a reintegration, and it should be done within theology?"

Lonergan: "The old distinctions were correct from an Aristotelian viewpoint but they are not from the viewpoint of method. And if one is going to have an integration, it can't be outside of theology."

Question 2:

"It seems that you say that religious conversion is non-conceptual (no insight) and non-judgemental. If this is so, how can religious conversion serve as the starting-point for a philosophy of God and systematics since these are based upon insight and judgements, as you so strongly aver in *Method in Theology?*"

Lonergan: "It is a basis insofar as it gives you a new horizon. It gives you the horizon in which questions about God are significant. There are people to whom you can talk about God and they listen eagerly. There are others who just react: 'What on earth is he talking about? How could I be interested in that?' Conversion is in Ezekiel: God plucking out the heart of stone. The heart of stone doesn't want to get rid of its stoniness. And that's the fundamental thing in religious conversion. I don't say there is nothing else happening, but I am saying that's what the key point is.

This key point you can have in all sorts of different contexts. It can be in the context of a hierophany: a god of the moment. In Shintoism there are, I believe, 800,000 gods. In other words, there have been 800,000 hierophanies: occasions of religious experience. A god can be the god of a person: the God of Jacob, or the God of Laban. A god can be the god of a group: the God of the Hebrews. And different religious experiences are terrifically varied. So the question arises, Is there something that is common to all of them?

I came across this question in the following manner. Wilfred Smith, about 1969, read a paper at the University of Toronto, saying that the historians of religion have done a terrific job of collecting and reporting all observable data connected with religion, but there remains a question: Why is it? What is religious commitment? What is it that makes religion change, transform, people's lives? And he thinks that is a question students of religion have to get after. There you have an example of a student of religion concerned with what is this fundamental thing, religious commitment.

And from there comes my method, the transcendental method: it's intentionality analysis at its root; you're starting from the subject and his operation. You can get a theological method if you have something further in the subject that will make that transcendental method into a theological method. And that is again religious experience, religious experience at its finest: God's gift of his love."

Question 3:

"Insofar as you regard the real possibility of the distinction of philosophy of God and religious experience, it seems you must presuppose that there's genuine religious consciousness to a degree apart from Christian revelation. But when you discuss religious consciousness, you do that chiefly with regard to the bible. Yet it seems to me that the bible would deny that there is a genuine religious consciousness apart from the revelation which it itself constitutes. Thus it seems to me that the bible would deny the possibility of the philosophy of God by your definition."

Lonergan: "Well, what about Paul's first epistle to Timothy, chapter two, verse four: 'God wills all men to be saved?'"

Question 3 (Continued): "The exegesis you give is the traditional Roman Catholic exegesis, but I think you'd be hard put to find that to be the genuine significance of that in any kind of literal sense. Paul is not really thinking that there must be grace bestowed on all men."

Lonergan: "I'm just stating what's said there."

Question 3 (Continued): "But Paul says in other places that unless the gospel is preached and unless the gospel is believed, all men will not be saved. So God is not providing the salvation of all men in any other way than to send his Son to whom the salvation of the world is owed."

Lonergan: "Well, that's another view, isn't it? But what Paul has to say about charity, that there isn't salvation without it—and there's lots of evidence of people leading extremely good lives without being Christians."

Question 3 (Continued): "But Paul never says charity is enough for salvation; for Paul it is faith in Jesus. Charity is the most important virtue, the most important response."

Lonergan: "Well, perhaps according to 'Paul.' It's an exegetical question. I was suggesting a line of thought. I am not doing detailed exegesis. Commonly theologians agree that God antecedently wills to save all men, and in I Cor 12, 3 Paul associates faith in Jesus with the gift of the Spirit and the absence of the Spirit with rejection of Jesus."

Question 4:
"With regard to the motives why you want to move natural theology over to systematic theology: is it that there are commitment–implications to a belief in God, a notional belief and a real belief in God involving action upon coming to the realization that God exists?"

Lonergan: "My fundamental reason for effecting the change is that when you have natural theology separate, most students when they come to theology will say, 'This is just more philosophy; it isn't religious; we don't want it.' That's a fundamental block in teaching theology. On the other hand, natural theology has a lot to gain from being in the context of a religious theology. And the abstraction that would separate the two is foreign to contemporary modes of thinking. We are not chopping up the world with a set of concepts and keeping it all in separate compartments. The main purpose is the development of the person, and the more one can put together, the more integrated the person will be."

Question 5:
"Returning to the common element to all religion: I assume this is the love of God. So you would call this in the old terminology supernatural revelation, not natural revelation?"

Lonergan: "Right. It isn't complete revelation. It isn't Christian revelation which is something which goes beyond it and thereby introduces a specific difference. There is an intersubjective element to love that is present in Christianity, inasmuch as God is expressing his love in Christ as well as giving you the grace in your heart, and this element is missing when the Incarnate Lord is missing."

Question 6:
"Daniélou has said that the Jewish-Christian revelation presents us with 'God in search of man,' whereas the other world religions speak of 'man in search of God.' Do you accept that?"

Lonergan: "No. I'd say with Pascal, 'You would not be seeking me unless you had already found me.'"

Question 6 (Continued): "God is always searching for man. Can you conceive of man in search of God?"

Lonergan: "Well, insofar as he is, it's because he has been given God's grace."

Question 6 (Continued): "He's always been given God's grace?"

Lonergan: "Yes."

2

THE FUNCTIONAL SPECIALTY, SYSTEMATICS

THE title of these lectures is *The Relationship between the Philosophy of God and the Functional Specialty, Systematics.* We have spoken about the philosophy of God. Our topic here will be the functional specialty, systematics. Following that, our concern will be the relationship between the two.

For the orientation of any that have not read chapter five of my book, *Method in Theology*, I feel I should say something about functional specialization. Very briefly, then, specialization is of three kinds. There is field specialization that divides the field of data into different parts so that each specialist concentrates on his part of the total field. There is subject specialization that divides the results of investigations into different subjects so that different professors give different courses on different subjects. Finally, there is functional specialization. It divides the process from data to results into different stages. Each stage pursues its own proper end in its own proper manner. The task of a method in theology is to distinguish between these proper ends and determine each of the proper manners of pursuing the proper ends.

The notion of functional specialization may be illustrated by the difference between experimental and theoretical physics. Only the experimental physicist can handle the cyclotron. But only the theoretical physicist can decide what experiments seem worth trying and, again, only the theoretical physicist can tell how significant the results of the experiment are. Similarly, the textual critic, the exegete, and the historian work on the same data but they perform quite different tasks. The textual critic studies the various readings found in the many manuscripts and citations in an effort to determine what the original text was. The exegete takes over to determine what the text originally meant. The historian takes over from several exegetes in the hope of arriving at an account of the course of events recounted in the manuscripts.

Now the notion of functional specialization is not entirely new in theology. In the past people were familiar with the distinction between dogmatic theology, concerned mainly with the doctrines defined by the church, and systematic or scholastic theology, concerned mainly with the meaning, significance, relevance of church doctrines. To these in more recent centuries were added positive or historical theology to meet the exigences of modern historical mindedness.

From these remarks you will correctly infer that theology is not the same thing as religion. Theology is reflection on religion. It mediates between a religion and a culture. Its function is to bring to light the significance and value of a religion in any given culture. It follows that, even though the religion remains unchanged, still a theology will vary with cultural variations.

So in *Method in Theology* eight functional specialties are distinguished. There is *research* to make available the relevant data. There is *interpretation* to ascertain their proper meaning. There is *history* to determine what was going forward in the past. There is *dialectic* to compare and evaluate the conflicting views of historians, the diverse interpretations of exegetes, the varying emphases of researchers. There is *foundations* that sets forth the horizon, the standpoint, that allows religious affirmations to have meaning and reveal values. There is *doctrines* that on the basis of foundations makes a selection from the alternatives presented by dialectic. There is *systematics* to clarify the meaning of doctrines. Finally, there is *communications* concerned with the task of preaching and teaching the doctrines to all men in every culture and in every class of each culture.

Of the eight functional specialties our concern here is only with the seventh, *systematics*. A first question that arises is how the Christian religion ever allowed itself to be involved in systematic thinking; after all, such thinking is not mentioned in the sermon on the mount. The answer is, of course, that it did so gradually. Let me briefly recall successive stages in the process.

In New Testament writings different layers may be distinguished. According to Reginald Fuller[7] a first layer corresponds to the gospel as it was preached to Jews that read the Old Testament in their native language. A second layer represents the gospel as it was preached to Jews that read the Old Testament in Greek. A third layer accords with the gospel as it would be preached to Gentiles that did not read the Old Testament at all. What differences resulted, Professor Fuller sets forth in successive chapters. But the point we would make here is that the New Testament bears witness to the fact that preaching the gospel to all nations necessitates preaching it differently to different nations. Cultural differences can be overlooked only at the cost of creating misunderstanding and misinterpretation.

Moreover, in the New Testament we also have a first adumbration of the distinction between philosophy of God and the functional specialty, systematics. The functional specialty presupposes revelation, as did the Jews that read the Old Testament. Philosophy of God does not use revelation as a logical premise for its conclusions, as did the Gentiles that did not read the Old Testament.

A further step was taken by the apologists of the second and third centuries. They had to take into account the pagans that accepted neither the Old Testament nor the New, that

[7] R. H. Fuller, *The Foundations of New Testament Christology*, New York: Charles Scribner's Sons, 1965.

misinterpreted Christianity, and persecuted Christians. The apologists' task was to make clear what Christians really believed and taught. To make it clear to pagans they had to enter into the mind of the pagans, to discern what they would accept as legitimate assumptions, and to proceed from that basis to a clarification of Christian doctrine. If you ask why the apologists were not content to preach the sermon on the mount, the answer is that the gospel can be preached by Christians only if Christians are allowed to exist. Justin Martyr was a second-century apologist. If one finds it strange that Justin wrote two apologies, at least one can infer from his martyrdom that he had some reason for his writing.

A third step arose in the interpretation of scripture. The fanciful interpretations proposed by the Gnostics had to be resisted, and the only successful way to resist them was to lay down the principles of hermeneutics and to apply them. Early in his *Miscellanies* Clement of Alexandria argued that the liberal arts of the Greeks along with philosophy came from God and, by philosophy, he meant not the Stoic or Platonic or Epicurean or Aristotelian school but a selection from them of what was correctly said and taught justice along with pious knowledge.[8] In the last book of the same work he presented a selection from the liberal arts when he explained how one is to determine the meaning of a text. He began from the Gospel precept: "Ask and you will receive; seek and you will find; knock and the door will be opened " (Mt. 7, 7; Lk. 11, 9). His application was to asking and answering questions relevant to the matter in hand in an orderly fashion without contentiousness or vaingloriousness.[9] He then went on to urge a methodical ordering of the questions asked, the definition of each of the words used, where the definitions were clearer than what they defined and were admitted by all. Once the words were defined, one was to determine whether or not any reality corresponded to the word. With that correspondence established one was to

[8] Clem. Alex., *Strom.*, I, 7; 37, 1.6; MG 8, 731 B and D; Stählin, II, 24.
[9] *Ibid.*, VIII, 1 ff.; MG 9, 558 ff.; Stählin, III, 80 ff.

nquire into the object's nature and its qualities. Further notes were added on proofs, signs, analysis, suppositions, general differences, species, categories, causes.[10] One has only to read a few samples of Gnostic exegesis to see that Clement had found the tool that would cut short many an endless disputation.[11]

A fourth step regarded one's apprehension of God. The Presocratic thinker, Xenophanes, had criticized the anthropomorphic gods of the Greeks and had remarked that, were they able to carve or paint, lions, horses, and oxen would represent their gods in their own image. The point was not lost on Clement of Alexandria who urged Christians to interpret not literally but allegorically the anthropomorphisms of the bible.[12] But if Christians were not to take the bible literally, then they had to have recourse to some other source for their notion of God. But for them this was no easy matter. Unless people are initiated philosophically, and not always then, they are unaware of the differences between the infant's world of immediacy and the adult's world mediated by meaning. Spontaneously they adopt the position of the naive realist with its materialistic implications. Readily they ask with Tertullian, Who will say that God is not a body?[13] Or with Irenaeus they conceive the omnipotent as the one that contains all the rest.[14] Or with Clement of Alexandria's *Excerpta ex Theodoto* they will argue that God the Father has a shape because the angels of little children contemplate his face and because the

[10] *Ibid.*

[11] See for example Irenaeus, *Adv. Haer.*, I, 3, 1.2; I, 3, 6; I, 8, 4; Harvey I, 24–26; 31; 75–78.

[12] Clem. Alex., *Strom.*, V, 11, 68, 3; V, 11, 71, 4; MG 9, 103 B and 110 A; Stählin, II, 371, 18 ff. and 374, 15. On Clement's interpretation of Xenophanes, see Bruno Snell, *The Discovery of the Mind*, New York: Harper (Torchbook), 1960, p. 142.

[13] *Tertullian's Treatise against Praxeas*, 7. Edited by Ernest Evans, London: S.P.C.K., 1948, p. 96 and see not on pp. 234 ff. Also M. Spanneut, *Le Stoïcisme des Pères de l'Eglise, De Clément de Rome à Clément d'Alexandrie*, Paris: Editions du Seuil, 1957.

[14] Irenaeus, *Adv. Haer.*, II, 1, 5; Harvey, I, 253 f.

pure of heart will see him.[15] Again, because he who sees the Father, they conclude that the Son is the face of the Father.[16] Further, since the devils suffer they must have bodies; angels are said to be without bodies only inasmuch as their bodies are less crass than ours; even the human soul is a body, otherwise Lazarus would be unable to dip his finger into water and place a drop on the tongue of the rich man in hell.[17]

In brief, ancient Christian writers had philosophic problems and gradually they discovered their existence. Irenaeus could conceive God in the Old Testament narrative style as the creator of heaven and earth, the producer of the garden of Eden, the author of the deluge, the God of Abraham, Isaac, and Jacob, the Father of Jesus Christ, the lord of the universe.[18] But he was aware in implicit fashion that, besides faith, there are also the preambles of faith. So he praised Justin Martyr because, in his book against Marcion, he had stated that he would not believe Christ if he had announced some god other than the creator and lord of all things.[19] So it was that Clement of Alexandria set about explaining how one should conceive God by abstracting from everything corporeal.[20] So Origen allied himself with the Middle Platonism to insist on the strict spirituality of the divine hypostases, of the angels, and of human souls.[21] It was a revision of the biblical notion of God that entailed a revision of the biblical notion of Christ, the controversies with Arians, Nestorians, and Monophysites, the emergence of a distinctive Christian apprehension of reality that

[15] Clem. Alex., *Excerpta ex Theodoto*, 11. Editions by R. P. Casey, London: Christophers, 1934, and by F. Sagnard, Paris: Les Editions du Cerf, 1948, Sources chrétiennes 23.

[16] *Ibid.*, 12.

[17] *Ibid.*, 14.

[18] Irenaeus, *Adv. Haer.*, II, 30, 9; Harvey, I, 368.

[19] *Ibid.*, IV, 6, 2; Harvey, II, 158 f.

[20] Clem. Alex., *Strom.*, V, 11, 71, 2.3.5; V, 12, 81, 5 ff.; Stählin, II, 374 and 382 f.

[21] Orig., *De princ.*, I, 1; Koetschau, 16–27; *In Ioan.*, IV, 21 ff.; Preuschen, 244 ff. But note the qualifications in *De princ.*, II, 2; Koetschau, 111, 28–113, 10.

had not been anticipated by Platonists or Aristotelians, Stoics or Gnostics.[22]

Though much profound thinking was expressed by the writers of the patristic era, it remains that theology did not seriously aspire to be systematic until the middle ages. Nor was that aspiration arbitrary. It arose out of the inner exigences of the situation. Theologians read; they were puzzled; they asked questions. Their finding was facilitated by anthologies, by books of sentences, by commentaries. Their questioning became an organized and ongoing procedure. Peter Abaelard in his *Sic et non* had argued from scripture, from patristic writings, and from reason that each of one hundred and fifty-eight propositions should be both affirmed and denied. Gilbert of Porrée advanced that there existed a question in theology when one proved from authority or from reason that the same proposition should be both affirmed and denied. This released a grand program of reconciliation. First, the existence of the question was to be proved by listing first the arguments against a proposition (*Videtur quod non...*) and then the arguments in its favor (*Sed contra est...*). Secondly, general principles of solution were to be presented (*Respondeo dicendum quod...*). Finally, the general principles were to be applied to each of the arguments alleged in proving the existence of the question (*Ad 1m, Ad 2m,...*).

The question, accordingly, was a technique for reconciling differing authorities in matters of faith and apparent oppositions between faith and reason. It could be applied to random issues, as in the Quodlibetal Disputations, when the master undertook to resolve any question that was raised. It could be applied to an orderly series of questions on a single topic, for example, to all the questions concerning truth or power or evil. It could be applied to all the questions that arose in reading a classified set of quotations from scriptural or patristic writings, such as were Peter Lombard's

[22] B. Lonergan, "The Origins of Christian Realism," *Theology Digest*, 20 (1972), 292–305.

Libri quattuor sententiarum. Finally, it could be applied to all the questions that arose in an account of the whole of Christian doctrine, as in Thomas Aquinas' *Summa theologiae.*

However, the larger the scale of the operations, the graver became a fresh problem. How was one to make sure that the many principles of solution that were proposed were themselves free from contradiction? The obvious solution was to derive one's principles of solution from some system. If the system was coherent, the solutions too would be coherent. If the system lacked coherence, this lack would be magnified in the solutions, and this magnification would lead to a correction of the system.

Now the simplest manner of moving from a common-sense to a systematic differentiation of consciousness is to adopt and perhaps also adapt a system that already exists. So it was that medieval theologians found in Arabic and Greek thinkers models for imitation and adaptation. Of these the most influential turned out to be Aristotle.

Still one cannot move from common-sense to systematic thinking without creating a crisis. One is introducing a new technical language, a new mode of formulating one's convictions and beliefs, a new mode of intellectual development, a new mode of verification. Automatically there is formed a new social group that understands the new technical language, that is expert in transposing from prior to later modes of expression, that is raising new questions and solving them in a new way. Automatically there also is formed a far larger social group that greets the new movement with incomprehension.

It happened that the spokesmen for the new group were largely Dominicans while those for the old ways were Franciscans. There was a knock-down controversy. John Peckham, who became archbishop of Canterbury in 1272, wrote to Rome that the doctrines of the two orders were opposed to each other on every debatable point, that one of these set aside and to some extent belittled the teachings of the saints, that it relied almost entirely n philosophic dogmas.[23] This, of course, was a plausible view rom a common-sense viewpoint. But what was going on, as ubsequent judgment would have it, was quite different. Aquinas lid not set Augustine aside or belittle him; he revered him, and us later works are more fully and accurately Augustinian than us earlier ones. Again, Aquinas did not derive his religious loctrine from Aristotle; he derived his religious doctrine from he Christian tradition, but he used Aristotle, partly as a master nd partly as a quarry, to construct a systematic presentation of Christian doctrine.

It is probable enough that thirteenth-century theologians could not have done better than turn to Aristotle for help. It remains hat Aristotle had his limitations. He conceived science as a deduc-ion of conclusions from necessary first principles. He believed uch principles could be reached empirically after the fashion in vhich a route ends in a rally; when one man makes a stand, others oin him, and still more come to their side.[24] But if this is a good llustration of the way in which insights accumulate and cluster o generate a discovery, still what is discovered is not a necessary ruth but a postulate or a hypothesis. Moreover, he wanted the oasic terms and relations of the sciences to be further determinations of the basic terms and relations of metaphysics. He was not ufficiently on his guard against a tendency to attempt to transform common-sense meaning into a systematic meaning by adding he qualifier "as such," *qua tale, kath' hauto*. Finally, he was quite unacquainted with relatively recent scholarship in hermeneutics nd in history.

Let us now attempt a thumbnail sketch of subsequent develop-ments. Ecclesiastical decrees in Paris and Canterbury banned the

---

[23] F. Ehrle, "John Peckham über den Kampf des Augustinismus und Aristotelismus in der zweiten Hälfte des 13. Jhs.," *Zeitschrift für Katholische Theologie*, 13 (1889), 181. The relevant passage has been quoted in my *De Deo Trino*, Rome: Gregorian Press, 1964, II, 49.

[24] Aristotle, *Post. Anal.*, I, 2, 71b 8–12; II, 19, 100a 11 ff.

constructive genius of Thomas Aquinas who had operated within the methodical mould of *lectio* and *quaestio*, a genuinely scientific method that arose and was developed spontaneously in the high middle ages. Aquinas took *lectio* seriously. He wrote commentaries on numerous books in the Old and New Testaments, on many of Aristotle's works, on the pseudo-Dionysius, on Al Farabi in whose writing he recognized a representation of the *Elementatio theologica* of Proclus. His familiarity with the whole of Aristotle protected him from any illusions that might be generated by the *Posterior Analytics*. In his *Contra Gentiles* he distinguished between matters in which both faith and reason could have a say and others in which faith alone was the issue. The former were treated in the first three books and they included man's naturally desired end, the beatific vision, and the external and internal means to that end, the law and the gift of grace. The latter were treated in the fourth book; they were trinity, the incarnation, original sin, and the sacraments. In the first three books not only demonstrative but also probable arguments were to be employed. In the fourth book the objections of adversaries were to be resolved, and probable arguments were to be adduced to confirm the faithful in their beliefs.[25]

When one turns from this cool implementation of faith's search for understanding, an understanding that may be certain or merely probable, to the writings of John Duns Scotus or William of Ockham, one finds oneself in a quite different world. They were by-products of the Augustinian–Aristotelian conflict. They accepted Aristotle's logical works. His other writings they disregarded as merely pagan. In consequence they took the *Posterior Analytics* at face value. Their basic concern was whether or not this or that issue could be settled demonstratively. When that approach combined with questions on what could be by God's absolute power, the one way to certitude was through the principle of

[25] *C. Gent.*, I, 13 No. 3.

non-contradiction. For absolutely God could do anything that did not involve a contradiction. There is no contradiction between the occurence of a hallucination and the absence of the hallucinated object.[26]

But the Augustinian–Aristotelian conflict left its mark on all schools. Father Congar has expressed surprise that Scotist vocabulary became the vocabulary of subsequent Scholasticism.[27] But clarity and rigor, though they may convey little understanding, at least are great advantages in a debate, and it was the debate that roused interest and passion. Today with our concern for sources we may be amazed that Capreolus wrote his commentary, not on the Lombard's *Sentences*, but on Aquinas' *Scriptum super sententiis*. Still stranger was Cajetan's commentary on the purely systematic work, the *Summa theologiae* of Aquinas. Was not theology painting itself into a corner?

A new orientation arose from the reformation and from humanism. The reformation gave us the council of Trent and Bellarmine's *De controversiis*. Humanism gave us Melchior Cano's *De locis theologicis*. The latter insisted on a return to sources. Theology was to consist in a set of medieval doctrines to be proved by an appeal to scriptural and patristic writings, to the councils and the consensus of theologians, and from *ratio theologica*, which sought to transform the ancient *fides quaerens intellectum* into an argument that did not prove. Perhaps more than a century passed before it became dominant, but the influence of Cano's *De locis* has extended right into the twentieth century.

Melchior Cano died in 1560 and his *De locis* was published posthumously. But in the last four hundred years the notions of science, of philosophy, and of scholarship have radically changed.

---

[26] Frederick Copleston, *A History of Philosophy*, Garden City, New York: Doubleday, 1963. III, 1, p. 77. Cf. *DS* 1033, 1948.

[27] Yves Congar, *A History of Theology*, ed. and trans. Hunter Guthrie, Garden City, New York: Doubleday, 1968, pp. 130 f.

Where Aristotle conceived science as a permanent acquisition of truth, our contemporaries conceive it as an ever fuller understanding of the data and so an ever closer approximation to truth. Where Aristotle conceived philosophy as basically a metaphysics whence all other disciplines derived their basic terms and basic relations, philosophy today in my opinion is basically a cognitional theory whence all other disciplines are able to derive an explicit account of their methods. Where Aristotle had only a perfunctory notion of hermeneutics and no serious concern for history, our contemporaries are eminent in the practice both of hermeneutics and of history.

It is the development of modern hermeneutics and history that has forced Catholic theology out of the manualist tradition. The old style dogmatic theologician was expected to establish a series of propositions, theses, from the Old Testament and the New, from patristic writings and the consensus of theologians, and from the *ratio theologica*. But modern scholarship set up an endless array of specialists between the dogmatic theologian and his sources. With the specialists the dogmatic theologian just could not compete. Without an appeal to his sources the dogmatic theologian had nothing to say. Such has been a basic and, as well, a most palpable element in the crisis of contemporary Roman Catholic theology. Along with the changes in the notion of science and the notion of philosophy, it has been my motive in devoting years to working out a *Method in Theology*.

It is only on the basis of a full understanding and a complete acceptance of the developments in the contemporary notions of science, philosophy, and scholarship, that my account of the functional specialty, systematics, can be understood, let alone accepted. Similarly, it is only on the basis of a full acceptance of the developments in contemporary notions of science, philosophy, and scholarship that there can be understood, let alone accepted, my proposal that philosophy of God be taught by theologians in a department of theology.

My aim, of course, is not to disqualify philosophers from aching or speaking about God. My aim is to qualify theologians r a task that once was theirs, that subsequently ceased to be .eirs, and once more I believe should become theirs.

The reasons for this belief is that changes in the notion of ience, philosophy, scholarship, and theology require adjust- ents. Former views were Aristotelian. They took for granted at the basic discipline was metaphysics and that other disciplines ad to derive their basic terms and relations by adding further terminations to the basic terms and relations of metaphysics. hey took for granted that each discipline had its field defined y a material object and its approach defined by a formal object. hey conceived theology as the science about God and about all thers things in their relation to God. They were taken by surprise y modern methods in exegesis and in history and put up a pro- acted resistance to them.

That resistance has ended. But there are other no less important hanges. The basic discipline, I believe, is not metaphysics but ognitional theory. By cognitional theory is meant, not a faculty sychology that presupposes a metaphysics, but an intentionality nalysis that presupposes the data of consciousness. From the ognitional theory there can be derived an epistemology, and :om both the cognitional theory and the epistemology there an be derived a metaphysics. These three are related to all other isciplines, not by supplying them with elements for their basic :rms and relations, but by providing the nucleus for the formu- ation of their methods. Instead of speaking of material objects ne speaks of data, and instead of speaking of formal objects one imply applies to the data the operations prescribed by the method. While theology used to be defined as the science about God, oday I believe it is to be defined as reflection on the significance nd value of a religion in a culture. From this view of theology : follows that theology is not some one system valid for all times nd places, as the Aristotelian and Thomist notion of system

assumes, but as manifold as are the many cultures within whic
a religion has significance and value.

The proposal, then, that philosophy of God be treated alon
with the functional specialty, systematics, does not stand alone.
is not a proposal that presupposes the notion of philosophy pro
sented to me as a student forty-five years ago or the notion o
theology presented to me as a student thirty-eight years ago. O
the contrary its suppositions are a radical revision of those notion
There is supposed a notion of science based, not on the extra
scientific notions of science assumed by modern scientists, but o
the analysis of scientific practice presented in the work, *Insigh*
There is supposed a notion of philosophy that is in accord wit
the achievements of modern science, that can ground the metho
of modern science, that does not attempt to dominate scienc
by telling it what its basic terms and relations must be. There
supposed a notion of theology that integrates a religion with th
culture in which its functions, that conceives the formal objec
of a theology by stating its method, that integrates within theolog
and its method what formerly were conceived as merely auxiliar
disciplines. Textual criticism and the edition and indexing o
texts used to be considered merely auxiliary disciplines, but i
Method in Theology they are regarded as the functional specialty
research. Exegesis once was considered to be an auxiliary disci
pline, but in *Method in Theology* it is regarded as the functiona
specialty, interpretation. History once was considered an auxiliar
discipline, but in *Method in Theology* it is regarded as the functiona
specialty, history. Doctrines regarding the divine legate, the churc
the inspiration of scripture once were considered to be funda
mental theology, but in *Method in Theology* these doctrines alon
with all others are included in the functional specialty, doctrine
while their foundational function has been handed over to th
evaluations and decisions of the functional specialties, dialecti
and foundations. Philosophy used to be regarded as the *ancill*
theologiae, the handmaid of theology; it happens however that th

handmaid for some centuries has gone in for women's liberation, and so in *Method in Theology* the philosophy that the theologian needs is included in the first four chapters on Method, The Human Good, Meaning, and Religion. Finally, what in Aquinas were considered probable arguments for the truths of faith or reasons for confirming Christians in their faith, in a later age became proofs from theological reason. In *Method in Theology* they are placed in the functional specialty, systematics, and its function is not to prove but to endeavor to find some understanding of the propositions established as true in the preceding functional specialty, doctrines.

I have mentioned these differences to obviate objections. My proposal to unify philosophy of God and the functional specialty, systematics, is not compatible with what everyone used to hold about textual criticism, exegesis, history, fundamental theology, philosophy, and theological reason. My proposal is compatible with quite different views. It is only the latter compatibility that I shall bother to defend.

QUESTIONS AND ANSWERS

Question 1:
"Cannot man by his own volition and free will separate himself from the love of God?"

Lonergan: "Yes, he can. Connected with it is one of the fundamental problems on grace. His separating himself of his own free will from the love of God is simple fact. But it is not explicable, for sin is an irrational; there is no explanation of why he does it. It's just revolt; but it can happen."

Question 2:
"Can the denial of existence render existence invalid? That is, can the absolute refusal to accept the existence of God in fact render the power of God's love impotent?"

Lonergan: "A person can be confused. If his negation of God's existence is that he can't prove it, or that the notion of God presented to him is not a satisfactory notion and he's rebelling against that unsatisfactory notion, he can be what Rahner would call an 'anonymous Christian,' a person who is in the state of grace but doesn't express himself the way people in the state of grace usually do. In other words, God's gift of his love is just that. It leads to a transformation in life, but more on the order of practice than on the order of intellectual knowledge. There are interpretations, for example, of Buddhism that consider that their atheism really isn't atheism at all—that they are mystics and they have no way of expressing their mystical experience except by denying the existence of God. This question can be extremely complex. We musn't expect people's lives—concrete living—to be coherent. It's a tendency towards coherence."

Question 2 (Continued): "Can a man's refusal bring the power of God's love to a screeching halt?"

Lonergan: "Insofar as it's sinful. He's refusing God's love and its advantages."

Question 2 (Continued): "So where he exists there is sort of a blank?"

Lonergan: "Well, no. It's just that he is not acknowledging God's existence. He no longer has the gift of God's love. It's the opposition—being in the state of grace and being in the state of mortal sin."

Question 2 (Continued): "That's not rendering God's love impotent?"

Lonergan: "No, that's not the proper way to put it. If you don't want to love in return, that at least for the moment ends that initiative on God's part. There is this mysterious thing sin, as well as this mysterious thing God's grace, and they are opposites."

Question 3:
"Is not the plucking out of the heart of stone in religious conversion a two-sided affair? The man must want it or it can't happen?"

Lonergan: "If it happens, the man will want it, simply because his heart is a heart of flesh. The man that didn't want it is the man who had a heart of stone. And that is the doctrine of the priority of God's grace."

Question 3 (Continued): "Can it remain a heart of stone if God plucks it?"

Lonergan: "Not then and there, no—if it has occurred. But God can do it and the man can refuse it. Then you have the surd of sin coming in."

37

Question 4:

"You say in you lecture that 'being in love does not presuppose or depend on any apprehension of God.' In *Method in Theology* you cite Rahner's statement to the effect that 'consolation without a cause' means 'consolation with a content but without an object' (p. 106, n. 4). Could you explain more precisely what this content without an object is?"

Lonergan: "The content is a dynamic state of being in love, and being in love without restriction. It's conscious but it's not known. What it refers to is something that can be inferred insofar as you make it advance from being merely conscious to knowing. And then because it's unrestricted, you can infer that it refers to an absolute being. But the gift of itself does not include these ulterior steps. They are further steps and consequently this content without a known object is an occurrence, a fundamental occurrence, the ultimate stage in a person's self-transcendence. It's God's free gift. It involves a transvaluation of values in your living, but it's not something produced by knowing. It's going beyond your present horizon; it's taking you beyond your present horizon."

Question 4 (Continued): "There would be no insight, no concept, no judgment?"

Lonergan: "Not of itself, no. You can say it's on the fifth level. It's self-transcendence reaching its summit and that summit can be developed and enriched, and so on. But of itself it is permanent."

Question 5:

"Can mystical works such as St. John of the Cross's *Spiritual Canticle* and *Living Flame of Love* be said to be the result of insight, since they are not the content of mystical experience but the content of reason seeking to articulate what transcends pure speculative understanding? In other words, do insights occur on the speculative level when the intellect tries to express what the soul has experienced mystically? In terms of Chapter XIX of

Insight ['General Transcendent Knowledge'] how could insights be said *not* to occur when reason attempts to formulate in language the content of mystical experience of the Transcendent?"

Lonergan: "There's mystical experience of the transcendent. There's the effort to say what's happening, to find out what's happening: 'Am I going nuts?' People with that experience are profoundly disturbed and they can be very apprehensive."

Question 5 (Continued): "Aren't you making an object out of content now?"

Lonergan: "Yes, you are discovering it. There isn't an already apprehended object. But you can find the object by reflecting and that reflection involves insight, and so on. The *Living Flame of Love* or the *Spiritual Canticle* is like any other writing—a matter of experience and understanding and judgment and verbal creativity. But that doesn't mean that the mystical experience itself is that. It's one thing to have the experience. It's another thing to describe it and express it and talk about it and evaluate it."

Question 6:
"You identify three questions that one might ask: Cognitional theory: What are you doing when you are knowing? Epistemology: Why is doing that knowing? Metaphysics: What do you know when you do it? How does question two differ from questions one and two? It would seem to add nothing to them. Is it not the same to ask: What are you doing when you are knowing? and to ask: Why is doing that knowing?"

Lonergan: "After you have answered the first question, knowing has taken on a different meaning. It means performing this set of operations. Why is performing this set of operations something relevant to knowing an independent reality? Why are the immanent criteria in your operations—the requirement to attend, to be intelligent, to be reasonable—what on earth have they to do with my ability to know something that is totally different from

39

myself? That's the epistemological problem. When we talk about knowing, what precisely happens when one is doing mathematics, when one is doing empirical science, when one is using one's common sense? Those are the questions in cognitional theory. The epistemological question is why these operations possess any relevance to knowing. And here you get to another question about knowledge: the validity of knowledge. The first is concerned with what occurs, the occurrence, an accurate account of what occurs when you are coming to know. You next reflect on that series of occurrences and ask: 'Is that really knowledge? Is it valid?'—the question that was raised by Descartes and Kant. The third question goes beyond the other two: What is the basic heuristic structure of everything that you are going to know?"

Question 7:

"Since you stress that it is conversion and not proof which is most crucial for the Christian, and since you are putting natural theology within the specialty, systematics, whose aim is not to prove anything, does the idea of actually trying to prove the existence of God really make any sense in our contemporary culture?"

Lonergan: "The objection is very logical. The whole idea of method is that we take all the means to attain an end. When I propose that philosophy of God be included, be taken along with systematics, I don't mean that it's ceased to be philosophy of God. I mean that the two cooperate, reinforce each other, have a common origin and a common goal. It's a performative unity; it's not a logical unity. It's not systematics dictating philosophy of God or philosophy of God dictating systematics. But it is mutual support, mutual clarification, each doing its own thing but at the same time helping each other."

Question 7 (Continued): "Won't the proofs that you work out through reason in natural theology seem pale compared to the conviction you already have through conversion?"

Lonergan: "Proof is never the fundamental thing. Proof always presupposes premises, and it presupposes premises accurately formulated within a horizon. You can never prove a horizon. You arrive at it from a different horizon, by going beyond the previous one, because you have found something that makes the previous horizon illegitimate. But growth in knowledge is precisely that.

There are proofs for the existence of God. I formulated them as best I could in chapter nineteen in *Insight* and I'm not repudiating that at all. But I say it's not a matter of comparing the two; it's using the resources of both. It's not letting the student of theology brush aside all systematic theology because, 'That's just more philosophy and we have wasted enough time on that already.' Similarly, there would be the theologian brushing aside philosophy because that doesn't presuppose the scriptures."

Question 7 (Continued): "Or a convinced Christian brushing aside both?"

Lonergan: "Yes."

Question 8 :
"You said you were going to speak about some of the problems of the philosophy of God. What is God?"

Lonergan: "It's something that most people know about. St. Thomas has five arguments for the existence of God. One from the first Mover. And he proves there is a first Mover, and he says that is what everyone means by God. He's presupposing a notion of God. And he does it for the second argument and for the third; he has something different for the fourth and the fifth. He identifies the conclusion with what everyone considers to be God. That, to my mind, is the fundamental notion of God and it's resulting from God's gift of his love.

Now you can go on and ask further questions on the basis of that knowledge and you can proceed to answering those questions, either along the lines of philosophy of God, natural theology, or along the lines of systematic theology. And the two are complementary. Take Thomas' *Theological Summa*. There he treats God as one—questions 2 to 26; in questions 30 to 43 he treats God as three persons. But in questions 27 to 29, he's preparing the fundamental elements of his trinitarian doctrine about God. He asks, 'Are there processions in God? Are there relations in God? Are these relations persons?' He's effecting the transition out of a natural theology into a systematic theology.

The two just marvelously fit together, and to want to pull them apart just creates repetitions. You can do philosophy of God in a philosophy department for people who aren't going to do theology later on. But if people are going to do theology, too, I'd say why break that up? That's my point."

Question 9:
"You have spoken of 'primitive language.' You're approaching it from a very philosophical standpoint. Most anthropologists would say that what you say is subjectively wrong."

Lonergan: "My source is *Philosophy of Symbolic Forms* by Cassirer."

Question 9 (Continued): "He's not an anthropologist. If you approach this particular problem which you're dealing with in these lectures in a purely philosophical way and ignore the social sciences, aren't you at the very same time undermining the theory of conceptualization?"

Lonergan: "I did not notice Cassirer ignoring the anthropologists. But the fundamental issue is to form notions about language so that you will have the tool, the models, when you come to do the empirical side of the study. There's an intelligibility that can be reached that way. It eliminates an awful lot of occult entities that obfuscate thinking. You'll find that point elaborated in the last section of my third chapter on Meaning in *Method in Theology*.

It's not at all a matter of brushing people aside; it's to set up a heuristic structure within which specialists in different fields can construct models that will help people enter into mentalities quite different from their own. Simple description does not suffice. There are fundamental tools that underlie language and that account for differences in languages and in the development of languages. The empirical study can be helped by this, or you can start from the empirical and move up to it. But if you move up to it, you'll move not into speculative philosophy, but cognitional theory."

Question 10:
"How would you define sin?"

Lonergan: "Mortal sin at the present time among moral theologians is, I believe, conceived in terms of fundamental option. There are fundamental options that are a turning against yourself, and against God, and against your neighbor. And that's what is meant by sin."

Question 10 (Continued): "What is the criterion for knowing what to do?"

Lonergan: The criterion for a value judgment is that it occurs in a virtuous person who pronounces the judgment with a good conscience. If you're vicious, you may have a good conscience when making a bad judgment. But if you're virtuous and make a bad value judgment, you will have a bad conscience. Such briefly is the criterion. I treat judgments of value in the chapter on the Human Good in *Method in Theology*."

Question 11:
"What about the criterion of the good conscience?"

Lonergan: "The good conscience means that, when you listen to an explanation, either you're satisfied or you put further questions. That satisfaction that comes from the act of understanding—or the dissatisfaction when you find the understanding inadequate

—is something that's immediate. Similarly, you often make a judgment. Metaphorically you marshal and weigh the evidence.

There is a more technical expression of that in the tenth chapter of *Insight*, but you know when your evidence is sufficient. A man comes home—he'd left his beautiful home in the morning, everything in perfect order—and he finds windows broken, water on the floor, smoke in the air. If he says, 'Something happened,' he knows he is absolutely right. If he says, 'There was a fire,' oh well, all of this could have been faked. And if he sees that, he won't say, 'There must have been a fire'—that is only a highly probable judgment.

And similarly the judgment of value in a good person reveals the truth insofar as it occurs with a good conscience and reveals its weakness by the uneasy conscience. Objectivity is the fruit of authentic subjectivity. All along the line, insofar as you are attentive, intelligent, reasonable, responsible, you will also be objective. They are the criteria. If you want to have something else, you'll box yourself up in some corner."

THE RELATIONSHIP BETWEEN PHILOSOPHY OF GOD AND THE FUNCTIONAL SPECIALTY, SYSTEMATICS

THERE are two issues. First, there is the basic issue of the viewpoint to be assumed in the discussion. Secondly, once the basic issue is settled, there is the detailed issue of working towards an account of the relationship between philosophy of God and the functional specialty, systematics.

The basic issue is between a static and a dynamic viewpoint. If the viewpoint is static, then from the very start everything really is settled. Nothing new can be added at any point after one has started. On the other hand, if the viewpoint is dynamic, then there can be added any number of reflections and discoveries that at the start were not included in one's assumptions.

The static viewpoint is the ideal of deductivist logic. One determines one's basic terms and relations. One determines how further terms and relations may be derived from the basic terms and relations. One sets forth one's postulates. One determines rules for valid inference. From this starting point, as a fixed basis, one proceeds. But all that one can discover is what one has already settled implicitly, for any conclusion one reaches must already be implicit in one's premises or else the result of faulty reasoning.

The dynamic viewpoint, on the contrary, is a moving

viewpoint. One starts from what one already knows or thinks one knows. One advances by learning what others have discovered and, perhaps occasionally, one may discover something for oneself. No limits are placed on what others or one oneself may discover. One's goal is not settled in advance. One may guess or make predictions, but it is not impossible that the guesses or predictions may prove mistaken.

Now this distinction between a static and a dynamic viewpoint is cardinal in our inquiry. If a static viewpoint is assumed to be the relevant viewpoint, then one is bound to conclude that philosophy of God and the functional specialty, systematics, are bound to be not only distinct but also separate. For if the static viewpoint is adopted, then both philosophy of God and the functional specialty, systematics, must be constructed in accord with the ideal of deductivist logic. But philosophy of God and the functional specialty, systematics, cannot form one and the same deductivist system. For one and the same deductivist system either does or does not have premises derived from a revealed religion. If it does, then philosophy of God is eliminated; and if it does not, then the functional specialty, systematics, is eliminated. It would seem, then, that if you mean to unite philosophy of God and the functional specialty, systematics, into a single deductivist system, then you are attempting the impossible.

But what is not possible from a static viewpoint may very well be possible from a dynamic viewpoint. The philosophy of God and the functional specialty, systematics, may have something in common in their origin and in their goal; each may go its separate way and yet, at the same time, each may borrow from the other and reinforce the other. While their procedures differ, this does not imply that they must be kept in different departments, treated by different professors, expounded in different books. While they cannot have the unity of a single deductivist process, they may very well have the unity of a single collaborative process.

Some, no doubt, may feel that to be content with a dynamic viewpoint and unity is to desert the notion of science properly so-called. But while I would grant that it does desert a narrow reading of Aristotle's *Posterior Analytics*, I think many would hesitate to agree that that narrow reading possesses any positive significance in the context of modern science, modern scholarship, or modern philosophy. Indeed, it would seem that only the older generation of contemporary theologians have any acquaintance with Aristotle's *Posterior Analytics* either in a narrow reading or the more intelligent reading that takes into account Aristotle's practice and even theory in his other works.

Indeed, if one accepts the theorem propounded by Kurt Gödel, one will conclude with him that realizations of the deductivist ideal are either trivial or incomplete or incoherent. They are trivial when their content is largely tautologous. They are incomplete when they lead to contradictory alternatives which they cannot resolve. They are incoherent when they demonstrate both the affirmation and the negation of the same proposition.

In brief, like the mortician, the logician achieves a steady state only temporarily. The mortician prevents not the ultimate but only the immediate decomposition of the corpse. In similar fashion the logician brings about, not the clarity, the coherence, and the rigor that will last forever, but only the clarity, the coherence, and the rigor that will bring to light the inadequacy of current views and thereby give rise to the discovery of a more adequate position.

The shift from the static to the dynamic viewpoint relativizes logic and emphasizes method. It relativizes logic. It recognizes to the fullest extent the value of the clarity, coherence, and rigor that logic brings about. But it does not consider logic's achievement to be permanent. On the contrary, it considers it to be recurrent. Human knowledge can be constantly advancing, and the function of logic is to hasten that advance by revealing clearly, coherently, and rigorously the deficiencies of current achievement.

I have said that the shift from the static to the dynamic viewpoint not only relativizes logic but also emphasizes method. For it is method that shows the way from the logically clear, coherent, and rigorous position of today to the quite different but logically clear, coherent, and rigorous position of tomorrow.

Method however can be conceived in quite different manners. Method can be thought of as a set of recipes that can be observed by a blockhead yet lead infallibly to astounding discoveries. Such a notion of method I consider sheer illusion. The function of method is to spell out for each discipline the implications of the transcendental precepts, Be attentive, Be intelligent, Be reasonable, Be responsible. Nor does the explicitness of method make the occurrence of discoveries infallible. The most it can achieve is to make discoveries more probable. The greater the number of investigators following a sound method, the greater the likelihood that someone will attend to the data that are significant. The greater the likelihood of attention focusing on the data that are significant in the solution of current problems, the greater the likelihood that the intelligent hypothesis will be proposed. The greater the likelihood of the intelligent hypothesis being proposed, the greater the likelihood of there being worked out the proper series of experiments to check and verify the hypothesis.

I have been contrasting a static and a dynamic viewpoint and I have been bringing the two together in a higher unity by urging that logic brings to each successive discovery the clarity, coherence, and rigor that will reveal the inadequacy of the discovery, while method shows the way from one discovery to the next. But while logic and method do enter into a higher functional unity, none the less a position that rests solely on the logical deductivist ideal without any awareness of the compensating values of method results in an extremely one-sided position.

For the man that knows his logic and does not think of method, objectivity is apt to be conceived as the fruit of immediate experience, of self-evident and necessary truths, and of rigorous inferences. When method is added to the picture, one may succeed in discovering that objectivity is the fruit of authentic subjectivity, of being attentive, intelligent, reasonable, and responsible.

For the man who knows his logic and does not think of method the basic discipline will regard objects generally. It will be a metaphysic. But when method is added to the picture, the basic discipline will regard not objects but subjects: it will be not a metaphysic but a cognitional theory; and the cognitional theory will provide the critical basis both for an epistemology and a metaphysic.

For the man who knows his logic and does not think of method, the relation of the basic discipline to other disciplines will be logical. The basic discipline will provide the basic terms and relations. The other disciplines will add further specifications to the terms and relations provided by the basic discipline. But when method is added to the picture, the relationship between the basic discipline and other disciplines lies in the field not of logic but of method. The basic discipline sets up a transcendental method, a manner of proceeding in any and every cognitional enterprise. The other disciplines add to transcendental method the categorial determinations appropriate to their specific enterprise.

For the man who knows his logic and does not think of method, the term "system" will have only one meaning. Systems are either true or false. True system is the realization of the deductivist ideal that happens to be true and, in each department of human knowledge, there is only one true system. But when method is added to the picture, three notions of system are distinguished. There is the mistaken notion of system that supposes that it comprehends the eternal verities. There is the empirical notion of system that regards systems as successive expressions of an ever fuller understanding of the relevant data and that considers the currently accepted system as the best available scientific opinion. Finally, there is system in the third sense that results from the appropriation of one's own conscious and intentional operations.

From these differences there arise different conceptions of theology. When the logical view prevails, theology is conceived as the science of God and of all things in their relation to God. As the methodical view develops, theology is conceived as reflection on the significance and value of a religion within a culture, and culture itself is conceived, nor normatively as though *de iure* there was but one human culture, but empirically and so with a full recognition of the many different manners in which sets of meanings and of values have informed human ways of life.

So much, then, for the preliminaries. I advocate the unity of the functional specialty, systematics, and of the philosophy of God, not on any and every set of assumptions, but only on one precise meaning of unity and only on certain assumptions concerning the meaning of objectivity, the content of the basic disciplines, the relationship between the basic and other disciplines, the nature of system, and the concept of theology. It is on these assumptions that I shall proceed to argue that the philosophy of God and the functional specialty, systematics, have a common origin, that each complements and reinforces the other, and that they have a common goal even though they proceed in different manners.

First, then, the two have a common origin in religious experience. Such experience varies with every difference of culture, class, or individual. But I have suggested on theological grounds that at the root of such experience is God's gift of his love. There is a gift of God's love that floods our inmost hearts through the Holy Spirit that God gives us (Rom. 5, 5). The acceptance of that gift of love is necessary for salvation (I Cor. 13). And God wills all men to be saved (I Tim. 2, 4). Further, I have argued that it is this gift that leads men to seek knowledge of God. God's gift of his love is God's free and gratuitous gift. It does not suppose that we know God. It does not proceed from our knowledge of God. On the contrary I have maintained that the gift occurs with indeed a determinate content but without an intellectually apprehended object. Religious experience at its root is experience of an un-conditioned and unrestricted being in love. But what we are in love with, remains something that we have to find out. When we find it out in the context of a philosophy, there results a philosophy of God. When we find it out in the context of a functionally differentiated theology, there results a functional specialty, systematics. So it turns out that one and the same God has unknowingly been found and is differently being sought by both philosopher and theologian.

Now it could be objected that the priority of a supernatural gift introduces a non-philosophic element with the result that philosophy of God ceases to be itself. Such a conclusion, I readily admit would follow on the assumption of the static viewpoint. For on that viewpoint objectivity is simply a matter of self-evident principles, immediate experience, and rigorous conclusions. To admit any other influence would be to rob pure reason of its purity. But what holds on the static viewpoint turns out to be ridiculous on the dynamic viewpoint. For there objectivity is conceived as the fruit of authentic subjectivity, and to be genuinely in love with God is the very height of authentic subjectivity.

Again, it may be objected that our position does not square with the decree of the first Vatican council to the effect that from the existence of creatures by the natural light of reason man can know with certainty the existence of God (DS 3004, 3026). Now I grant that this conclusion would follow if the decree meant that fallen man without grace can know with certainty the exis-tence of God. But most certainly that is not the meaning of the decree. For an earlier stage of the decree said precisely that, while the final version omitted both the words "fallen" and "demonstrated."[28]

[28] The third schema of the constitution, *Dei Filius*, in the corresponding canon read: "...per ea quae facta sunt, naturali ratione ab homine lapso certo cognosci et demonstrari posse...." J. D. Mansi, *Sacrorum conciliorum nova et amplissima collectio*, 53, 168. See also my article, "Natural Knowledge of God," *Catholic Theological Society of America Proceedings*, 23 (1968), 54–69.

Finally, may I point out once more the great advantage that accrues to philosophy of God when it is acknowledged to be seeking the same God as do the theologians and, indeed, as do all men for "...he is not far from each one of us, for in him we live and move, in him we exist...." (Acts 17, 27). It was Blaise Pascal that contrasted the god of philosophers with the God of Abraham, Isacc, and Jacob. That contrast has since been so extended that the god of the philosophers has become another god, a usurper, an idol. In such a climate of opinion it is of extreme importance to ascertain that it is one and the same God that unknowingly has been found though differently sought by both philosophers and theologians.

Our first point, then, has been that philosophy of God and the functional specialty, systematics, have the same source and origin in God's gift of his love. In both disciplines man is seeking to know whom he is in love with. Our second point will be that philosophy of God needs to stand in the context of the functional specialty, systematics. Here our basic argument will be that the question of God arises on a series of successive levels, that it may begin as a purely metaphysical question but it becomes a moral and eventually a religious question, and that to deal with all of these levels requires putting an end to the isolation of philosophy of God.

As I suggested in *Method in Theology*,[29] the basic form of the question of God arises when one questions one's questioning. Now our questioning is of different kinds. There are our questions for intelligence and by them we ask what, and why, and how, and what for. There are our questions for reflection and by them we ask is that so or is it not so, is it certain or is it only probable. There are our questions for deliberation and by them we ask whether what we are doing is really worthwhile, whether it is truly good or only apparently good. Finally, there is the religious question:

---

[29] See pp. 101–103.

we are suffering from an unconditioned, unrestricted love; with whom, then, are we in love?

A first form of the question of God may be derived from our questions for intelligence. Answers to such questions are reached when the desire to understand expressed in the question is met by the satisfaction of actually understanding. Still the desire to understand is not simply a desire for a subjective satisfaction. It wants more. It wants to understand the persons and things that make up one's milieu and environment. How is it, then, that the subjective satisfaction of an act of understanding can be the revelation of the nature of the persons and things in one's milieu and environment? Obviously, if intelligence can reveal them, they must be intelligible. But how can they be intelligible? Does not the intelligibility of the object presuppose an intelligent ground? Does not an intelligent ground for everything in the universe presuppose the existence of God? Such is a first form in which arises the question of God.

A second form of the question of God arises when we reflect on our questions for reflection. In my book, *Insight*, I concluded that answering questions for reflection supposes that we reach a virtually unconditioned. The meaning of this phrase "virtually unconditioned" has its simplest expression in the hypothetical syllogism, If A, then B; but A; therefore B. In the major premise, If A, then B, the consequent, B, is conditioned by A. In the minor premise, but A, the condition is fulfilled. In the conclusion, therefore B, there is posited the virtually unconditioned, namely, B was a conditioned but its condition has been fulfilled and so virtually it is unconditioned.

Now all the objects in our sensible universe are known only as virtually unconditioned. Their existence is not necessary but conditioned. They are contingent beings and so they can be known to exist only when their existence has been verified. But can everything be contingent? Must there not exist necessary being, whose existence is unconditioned, to account for the existence of the beings whose existence is conditioned? In this fashion there once more arises the question of God.

A third form of the question of God is had when one deliberates about one's deliberating. To deliberate is to ask whether this or that course of action is worthwhile. To deliberate about one's deliberating is to ask whether it is worthwhile ever to stop and ask whether one's course of action is worthwhile. No doubt, we are moral beings. No doubt, we are forever praising X and blaming Y. But the fundamental question is whether or not morality begins with the human race. If it does, then basically the universe is amoral; and if basically the universe is amoral, then are not man's aspirations to be moral doomed to failure? But if man is not the first instance of moral aspiration, if basically the universe is moral, then once more there arises the question of God. One asks whether the necessarily existing and intelligent ground of the universe also is a highly moral being.

A fourth form of the question of God arises when one reflects on religious experience. No doubt, such experience takes many forms. No doubt, it suffers many aberrations. But it keeps recurring. Its many forms can be explained by the many varieties of human culture. Its many aberrations can be accounted for by the precariousness of the human achievement of authenticity. Underneath the many forms and prior to the many aberrations some have found that there exists an unrestricted being in love, a mystery of love and awe, a being grasped by ultimate concern, a happiness that has a determinate content but no intellectually apprehended object. Such people will ask, With whom are we in love? So in the fourth and final manner there arises the question of God.

Now if the question of God arises on four different levels, it does not follow that there are four distinct and separate questions. The questions are distinct but they also are cumulative. The question of God is epistemological, when we ask how the universe can be intelligible. It is philosophic when we ask why we should bow to the principle of sufficient reason, when there is no sufficient reason for the existence of contingent things. It is moral when we ask whether the universe has a moral ground and so a moral goal. It finally is religious when we ask whether there is anyone for us to love with all our heart and all our soul and all our mind and all our strength.

It can quite plausibly be argued that the fourth question would not occur if man existed in the state of pure nature. In that case the philosophy of God would not only be distinct from the functional specialty, systematics, but that functional specialty would not exist. But man at present does not exist in the hypothetical state of affairs named pure nature. The question of God can be raised in all four ways. The four ways are cumulative. They belong together. So we should put an end to the practice of isolating from each other the philosophy of God and the functional specialty, systematics.

But further, one must not think that the question of God is fundamentally philosophic, that in the state of pure nature it would not extend into theological terrain, that accidentally in the present state of affairs it merely happens to move out of its proper sphere and touch on matters that are theological. The vast majority of mankind have been religious. One cannot claim that their religion has been based on some philosophy of God. One can easily argue that their religious concern arose out of their religious experience. In that case the basic question of God is the fourth question that arises out of religious experience. It is only in the climate of a philosophically differentiated culture that there occurs reflection on our questions for intelligence, our questions for reflection, and our questions for deliberation.

Finally, it is only in the climate of religious experience that philosophy of God flourishes. I do not think it difficult to establish God's existence. I do think it a life-long labor to analyze and refute all the objections that philosophers have thought up against the existence of God. But I see no pressing need for every student of religion to penetrate into that labyrinth and then work his way out. Much more necessary and also much more fruitful is the self-appropriation that grounds cognitional theory, epistemology, and metaphysics, that provides the criteria for distinguishing positions from counter-positions, that leads into an account of the human good, that extends into a general theory of meaning, that brings to light man's capacity for self-transcendence and the relation between that capacity and religion. Now such are the topics treated in the first four chapters of *Method in Theology*. They underpin the practice of theology. But they also underpin rational arguments that establish God's existence and attributes. It is in this climate of reflection on religion that philosophy of God acquires its significance and attains its proper effectiveness.

But if philosophy of God has much to gain by being joined by the functional specialty, systematics, it is no less true that the functional specialty has much to gain by the same union. For the categories employed by the theologian are both general and special. The special categories are employed only by theologians. The general categories are employed in other disciplines as well, in philosophy, in the sciences, in hermeneutics and history. For theology, insofar as it acquires a method, becomes a reflection on the significance and value of a religion within a culture; because it treats of religion, it has its own special terms; because it is concerned with the significance and value of the religion within a given culture, it has to have recourse to the general terms that refer to significance, value, and culture in their many aspects.

In brief, the world of the theologian is not some isolated sphere cut off from the affairs of men. But the static viewpoint inevitably leads to such isolation. By rejecting the static viewpoint, by conceiving theology as an ongoing process guided by a method, one puts an end to isolationism. The concern of the theologian is not just a set of propositions but a concrete religion as it has been lived, as it is being lived, and as it is to be lived. So conceived, theology has to draw on the resources not only of scientists and historians but also of philosophers.

It is true, of course, that dropping the static and accepting the dynamic viewpoint imply that one is setting aside the old-time notions of philosophy and theology. Logic ceases to rule the roost. The dominant issue is method. The possibility of method is a multiple differentiation of consciousness: the religious, the linguistic, the literary, the systematic, the scientific, the scholarly, and the self-appropriation of intentionality analysis. When all of these differentiations of consciousness have been achieved, the consequent notions of philosophy and theology are quite different from what they were when only the first four differentiations had occurred. For example, the Thomist and especially the neo-Thomist conceptions of philosophy and theology rest on the religious, the linguistic, the literary, and the systematic differentiations of consciousness. Commonly they are unfamiliar with the differentiations resulting from modern science, modern scholarship, and contemporary intentionality analysis.

The importance of the closest relationship between philosophy and theology in the present situation is revealed by the contemporary breakdown of scholasticism. People generally no longer accept or even consider a scholastic metaphysics. The consequence has been that they water down or reject the truths of their faith. This they excuse on the ground that the early church at Jerusalem, Antioch, Corinth, Rome had no interest in metaphysics. This they further excuse on the ground that they have no idea how there could be any development of revealed truth. But a lack of understanding proves nothing but one's own incompetence. Before one can judge whether or not a development of revealed truth is possible and legitimate, one had best understand how it could be conceived to be possible and legitimate. To communicate such an understanding cannot be attempted in the present paper. But at least a clue can be thrown out. The possibility of a development in doctrine arises whenever there occurs a new differentiation of consciousness, for with every differentiation of consciousness the same object becomes apprehended in a different and a more adequate fashion.

I have claimed that philosophy of God and the functional specialty, systematics, have a common origin and common objective: their origin is religious experience, and their objective is to discover its significance and estimate its value. I have argued that philosophic questions concerning God lead into strictly religious questions, and that the philosophic inquiry needs the support of the properly religious context for the full and effective attainment of its goal. I also have argued that the functional specialty, systematics, is concerned not only with the strictly supernatural but also with the effect of God's gift of his love on man's life and history in this world; hence the functional specialty not only has its own special and strictly religious categories but also the categories it shares with other fields and notably the ones it shares with philosophy. I have pointed out the havoc wrought on people's faith when their philosophy is jettisoned without being replaced. I have now to add a final consideration.

It has to do with the contemporary notion of person. The traditional view was the product of trinitarian and christological problems as these were conceived with the systematic differentiation of consciousness as originated by Aristotle and transposed to Christian soil by Thomas Aquinas. The contemporary view comes out of genetic biology and psychology. From the "we" of the parents comes the symbiosis of mother and child. From the "we" of the parents and the symbosis of mother and child comes the "we" of the family. Within the "we" of the family emerges the "I" of the child. In other words the person is not the primordial fact. What is primordial is the community. It is within community through the intersubjective relations that are the life of community that there arises the differentiation of the individual person.

It follows that "person" is never a general term. It always denotes this or that person with all of his or her individual characteristics resulting from the communities in which he has lived and through which he has been formed and has formed himself. The person is the resultant of the relationships he has had with others and of the capacities that have developed in him to relate to others.[30]

Now extremely relevant to the notion and the development of the person conceived in this fashion has been our conception of religious experience and our view of the philosophy of God and of functional specialty, systematics, as arising from religious experience and as aiming at its clarification. For the strongest and the best of the relationships between persons is love. Religious experience at its first root is the love of God with one's whole heart and whole soul, with all one's mind and all one's strength, and from it flows the love on one's neighbor as oneself. If persons are the products of community, if the strongest and the best of communities is based on love, then religious experience and the emergence of personality go hand in hand.

It follows that, as philosophy of God and the functional specialty, systematics, have a common origin in religious experience, so also they have a common goal in the development of persons. But each person is one, a whole, and not just a set of parts. It follows that the study of what makes persons persons is not to be carried on under different principles and in different departments. Philosophy of God and the functional specialty, systematics, may and should unite. They have a common origin; they complement and reinforce each other; they are concerned with the common goal, the promotion into clear consciousness of the major factor in the integration and development of the person.

[30] For much more on the topic see Maurice Nédoncelle, *La réciprocité des consciences, Essai sur la nature de la personne*, Paris: Aubier, 1942.

QUESTION AND ANSWERS

Question 1:
"How can you justify starting methodology with cognitional theory? Doesn't the basic judgment of existence underpin every act of perception, questioning, and affirming? Don't I implicitly affirm 'Something exists' from the beginning of my acts of awareness? If so, isn't metaphysics implicitly prior to cognitional theory?"

Lonergan: "Metaphysics is prior if you consider that what you're studying is fully known objects. In other words, it's dealing with objects. When you start out that way, you have no way of critically justifying your metaphysics. You can critically justify it if you derive it from a cognitional theory and an epistemology. And you can critically justify the cognitional theory by finding it in yourself: the terms of the theory are found in you own operations, of which you are conscious and which you are able to identify in your won experience, and the relations connecting the terms are to be found in the dynamism relating one operation to the other."

Question 1 (Continued): "Is that question presuming that there's a real disagreement between metaphysicians, one using the object, and the other seeing and using subjectivity as a proper means?"

Lonergan: "There's a fundamental difference inasmuch as the question supposes a position like Gilson's in his *Réalisme thomiste et critique de la connaisance* written in 1939. I discussed it in 'Metaphysics as Horizon,' the chapter in *Collection*, comparing Coreth, Gilson, and Kant."

Question 1 (Continued): "This then becomes a problematic among people like Maritain, Kant, and Rahner?"

Lonergan: "Yes, Rahner's philosophic position is expressed by Coreth in his *Metaphysics*, and what he begins with are the questions. He says there's a question about the starting point. Let's take the question as a starting point. Your knowledge of existence—'Is it so' is the first question you ever raise and if you do, you'll say, 'Something exists,' and it fits the affirmation something exists from the beginning of my acts of awareness.

You have that implicit if you need it. But you don't need it. Judgments result from sufficient evidence and sufficient evidence for something precise that's been conceived. So your questions for intelligence precede your questions for reflection, your judgment, and your experience has to precede your acts of understanding; otherwise you'll have nothing to be understood. But if you want to conceive human knowing as taking a look— What is it to know?—it's to take a good look. And what does your intellect do?—it takes an intellectual look at an abstraction. Gilson escapes from that by introducing this implicit judgment. An implicit judgment is a judgment that hasn't occurred yet."

Question 2:
"It seems you're liable to the charge of subjectivism. Could you explain 'authentic subjectivity,' a phrase you've been using in these lectures?"

Lonergan: "Subjectivity is authentic in the measure that it's attentive, intelligent, reasonable, responsible. Those are the conditions of being an authentic person. The thing is that our knowing is discursive. It's not intuitive; it is discursive. Until you have clear concepts, you can't observe.

Suppose there's a bug on a table—all I can say about it is that it's a bug. But an entomologist can tell you 150 or 200 things about it, and he can do so because he has the words and the concepts, and he's studied the thing carefully under all its aspects. I was once at a discussion in Los Angeles at Loyola of scientists and philosophers, and the question arose whether science kept on developing indefinitely. The chairman of the department of chemistry (this was almost ten years ago) said that in the last five years, theoretical discoveries in chemistry have enormously enlarged the data we can see. Until you have got understanding and clear concepts, you may feel a little ill at ease, but you don't really attend to the objects.

People talk about Maréchal. Maréchal was the one that effectively introduced in Catholic circles the notion that human knowledge is discursive and that you know when you affirm. An affirmation is a detail of the process, the third level. I was taught philosophy on an intuitive basis—naive realism—and I took refuge in Newman's *Grammar of Assent*. Later I read a book by J. A. Stewart, *Plato's Doctrine of Ideas*—it was a book that influenced me unconsciously a great deal. I discovered that, according to Stewart, Plato's ideas are what the scientist is trying to discover and what Plato is doing in the Dialogues is setting up a methodology."

Question 3:
"It seems, then, that the authentic Christian mystic is best suited to explore the meaning of God."

Lonergan: "The trouble with mystics is that they are not interested in any of these questions. They consider all these books rather silly and superfluous. They don't even want to read books on mysticism. While they have certain advantages—they're beautiful persons—you can't interest them in joining any investigation."

Question 3 (Continued): "What good are they to theology?"

Lonergan: "They're good to the Church. Luigi Sturzo has said that there are two components in the ongoing history of the Church—the organizational and the mystical. The mystical brings things to life again and the organization keeps them going even though you have no more mystics. When the need for more mystics becomes evident, then Divine Providence, we hope, will step in."

Question 4:
"In your writing you have stated that the present crisis of modern

man is not one of faith but of culture. I have taken this to mean that the shift in world views via the rise of modern science, and especially today in the social sciences, has made it difficult for modern man to understand his 'place' in the universe, and thus to properly order himself and his society. Yet the contemporary moves attacking human life, the family, and authority appear to me as perhaps not a cultural change but a godless—at best human-istic—movement which may best be met by Christian faith. Could you please clarify what you mean by this cultural shift we are witnessing?"

Lonergan: "What I'm talking about is a crisis in the Church, the crisis in the Church that involves radical change in theology brought on by the inadequacy of the philosophy and the scholarship and the notions of science that we had in the past. That's the fundamental problem in the Church at the present time. Fr. Andrew Greeley in his interview with a Bishop's committee after his sociological report said that the fundamental need is theory at the present time. The fundamental problem is not celibacy or faith, but theory, and that's what I'm saying. I'm not talking about the world problems.

The origins of this atheism and lack of faith are the eighteenth-century Enlightenment which through universal education has been communicated to the masses. In the general situation the emphasis made by the question is correct—namely, in the general field of human society. In general the eighteenth century wanted to get rid of positive religion, revealed religion, and to get rid of it they said, 'Let's get rid of tradition.' And when you get rid of tradition, you move back to the state of pre-Cro-Magnan man. There is a critis in our tradition today. It's a cultural crisis because it is affecting our tradition."

Question 5:
"If the possibility exists that man can separate himself from the love of God by his own free will, are men who possess a love for God made equally exposed to the elements that make up this potential separation?"

Lonergan: "St. Paul says, 'Make out your salvation in fear and trembling and pray for perseverance.' It's the thing to be prayed for, and therefore because it has to be prayed for, it's not something you already possess securely. Human authenticity is always precarious, but if you have the love of God in you heart you are that much better off. Aristotle said that virtues make you do the right thing promptly, easily, and with pleasure, and Aquinas said— 'Well, at least not with too much pain.'"

Question 6:
"What do you think of the concept of God derived from process philosophy? Is a god who changes in perfection compatible with the Christian notion of God discussed in systematics, or the philosophical notion of God in *Insight*?"

Lonergan: "Everyone admits that there are contingent predications of God: things that are true about God and not necessarily true. God created the world and he needn't have created the world. This is a contingent predication about God. Does that imply that there's a real change in God? If you are a process philosopher you'll say yes, and if you're not one you'll say no. The question is, Is the metaphysics of God the same as the metaphysics about man? If you make a new decision, there's a real change in you. If God decides to create a world, is there a real change in him? Is the metaphysics of an infinite being the same as the metaphysics of a finite being? That's the fundamental form of the question.

Now the concept of God in *Insight* is a concept of an unrestricted act of understanding, an absolute intelligibility. In Whitehead's *Process and Reality* God is the first accident. There is a radical opposition there because an accident is something that is not intelligible; it just happens. The questions concerned with the basis of the contingent predication about God started out in Aristotle where with Aristotle the action is in what's moved, not in the mover. The mover doesn't change; it's what moves that changes. If no one is learning, you are not doing any teaching, because teaching and learning are the same thing. It's the thing in the person that learns, but it's from the person that teaches.

Sound and hearing are the same thing. The bell can put longitudinal waves in the air, but that's not sound. Sound is what's in potency in the ear when there's nothing ringing, and what actually is in the ear when something is ringing. But it's sounding insofar as it's from the bell and it's hearing insofar as it's in you. You have there a first instance in which predications imply not a reality in the agent, but a reality in the effect.

And that's the basis of the Thomist doctrine that creation is a notional relation in God and a real relation in us. There are shifts in terminology when you move from one to the other. That is just a rough outline. I can go on to the question of understanding and willing, and so forth, whether those predications are the same. God's an infinite being—what do you add to him? With regard to God as undergoing change in the course of time—it's an anthropomorphic conception of God, God being more like us. It conceives God not as a God of the universe but as part of the universe: an accident within the universe."

Question 6 (Continued): "Have process philosophy and process theology any sure role to play in our own development of thought?"

Lonergan: "We have to get over the notion that metaphysics is static: what's static is logic. There are conceptions of substance that are ludicrous, and often current. There's a purification of metaphysical concepts that is needed that process philosophy attempts. I don't think that they have succeeded in effecting the purification that they want."

Question 7:
"Suppose I were a philosopher with a well worked out philosophy of God and a theologian with a highly developed systematics— what further developments would be open to me?"

Lonergan: "Well, you can go on to communications, expressing what you have acquired to people in every class and in every culture, or at least getting to know one class of some culture very well and saying it to them. And communications is not simply a matter of one person doing something. What is the church? The church is a process of communication, an ongoing process, of the message of the Gospel, of that message that is what the Christian knows, of the content that informs his life and of the precepts that guide his actions. That communication is the fruit, the final stage of theology; it's the eighth of the functional specialties."

Question 8:
"In light of your ideas of 'I' and 'We' and the artificial means of birth being developed—test tube babies—do you think this technology would be dehumanizing?"

Lonergan: "Without the love of the parents the infant is retarded. I think the psychologists will agree with that. You don't get mother's love in an incubator. There is not developed the attachment the mother has to her own child. She has not carried that child. There's a psychological dimension to it."

Question 9:
"If authentic subjectivity is a prerequisite to environment, then to what extent does that subjectivity not also become content, or a product, of the inquiry and then how, if it is content or product, can my inquiry be communicable to you subjectively?"

Lonergan: "Subjective doesn't mean anything distinct from objective; it's the source of objectivity. How one person understands another person is an extremely complex process. Learning new words, catching on to new uses of words—you make the gesture, someone else interprets it; you see the corrections you should make in your gesture to get him to understand what you really mean. The gestures can be made manually or vocally or anything else. That's the communication side.

Your inquiry doesn't presuppose authentic subjectivity. The roots of authentic subjectivity are already there in your attentiveness, intelligence, reasonableness, and responsibleness. That's the source of your questions, on these different levels. Subjectivity, insofar as it accepts mistaken notions, beliefs, is distorted, and it has to work itself out of a blunder, and correcting errors is not easy. But there is a process: by muddling through you can get there. Your position is a rather static one, wanting logical explanations for everything."

Question 10:
"This question arises out of my religious experience. With whom am I in love? Do I go back to another level when asked another question that arises out of my religious experience?"

Lonergan: "You're going back to a speculative level. That was Anselm's question. The religious experience of the Christian is specifically distinct from religious experience in general. It's intersubjective. It's not only this gift of God's love, but it has an objective manifestation of God's love in Christ Jesus. That intersubjective component creates a difference and because it creates a difference, insofar as you advert to that intersubjective element in you love with Christ, you're proceeding from experience. Your question is coming out of your experience. It's insofar as you are related to Christ as God."

Question 11:
"Does what you have said have any bearing on the relationship between the functional specialty of doctrines, for example, the Christian teaching about God, and the systematic understanding of God? What is the distinction between those two?"

Lonergan: "Doctrines is the previous functional specialty. All eight interact, but conception of them is sequential. Doctrines come out of a dialectic that lines up the differences between historians, interpreters, researchers, and reduces those differences to their roots. You have opposed positions and counter-positions coming out of dialectics. Foundations give you the horizon within which religious statements have a meaning. By applying foundations to dialectics you get doctrines. In systematics you can say: What does this mean?"

Question 11 (Continued): "In doctrines do you get a statement about God in which you have no understanding of the meaning of it?"

Lonergan: "You have some understanding; you have a catechetical understanding of it. Or you can have an historical understanding, insofar as you have been studying the history."

INDEX